How Bullfrog Found His Sound

By Eric Michaels
Illustrated by Susan Edison

Modern Curriculum Press

Modern Curriculum Press
299 Jefferson Road, P.O. Box 480
Parsippany, NJ 07054-0480

Internet address:
http://www.mcschool.com

Design by Agatha Jaspon

ISBN: 0-7652-0888-1

1 2 3 4 5 6 7 8 9 10 MA 05 04 03 02 01 00 99 98

CONTENTS

Chapter 1
Bullfrog's Problem

Once, long ago, a cheerful young bullfrog sat on a log in a swamp. Above him the moon was full and bright. Around him the night was strangely quiet.

The still night made Bullfrog feel uneasy. The swamp was usually noisy. But tonight, something dangerous was in the air.

Bullfrog took a few deep breaths. "Maybe I'll hum a little tune," said Bullfrog.

"Hmm, hmm," rasped Bullfrog in his croaky voice. Bullfrog loved to use his voice. Humming and croaking were two of his favorite things to do. Humming usually made Bullfrog feel better when he was upset. But on this clear moonlit night, Bullfrog was still uneasy.

"Maybe I'll try a little croaking," thought Bullfrog. "Perhaps a friend will hear me. Then I'll have someone to talk to."

"RIBBIT! RIBBIT!" he called.

No other frogs croaked back. Bullfrog shifted on his log. He felt lonely and a little worried. "Where is everybody?" he wondered.

Then above him, Bullfrog heard the soft sound of wings whispering across the sky.

Swish! Swish!

A heron landed in a nearby tree.

The great blue heron settled on a branch right above Bullfrog.

"Hello, Heron," Bullfrog said as boldly as he could.

"Hello, Bullfrog," said Heron.

"Heron," said Bullfrog, "I was hoping for some company tonight. But I'm not sure you're the right kind of company for me. I've heard that you eat frogs for dinner!"

Heron gazed up at the moon. He thought for a minute. Then he looked down.

"Bullfrog," Heron said. "You are right. You seem like a very nice frog, but I am a very hungry bird. Although you would make fine company, dinner comes first. A nice fat frog like yourself is just what I am looking for!"

The last thing Bullfrog wanted was to be a meal for Heron! His mind raced. Bullfrog looked all around the moonlit swamp, searching for an idea. All he saw were the lacy shadows of trailing moss floating on top of the water. He saw the dark shadows of large rocks at the water's edge. Not another creature was in sight. Everyone had scurried into nests, holes, and logs with Heron in the neighborhood.

Bullfrog was a smart frog. But he couldn't think of any really good ideas.

"Heron," said Bullfrog weakly, "if you fly around the swamp, I'm sure you'll find plenty of smaller frogs to eat. They will taste much better than I will."

Heron laughed. "Bullfrog," he said, "you are not fooling me. I know that bigger frogs are tastier frogs. Besides, no other frogs are around. You need to think of a better reason why I should not eat you."

"Heron," Bullfrog said, "just look at me! I'm a very special frog. No other frog in the swamp is quite like me."

Bullfrog puffed himself up so that he was as big and as round as a ball. He even tried to smile, which was not an easy thing for a puffed-up bullfrog to do. Heron stared at Bullfrog with keen eyes and inspected him carefully. He saw a large yellowish-green frog with brown markings. He saw long legs and a white belly.

"Bullfrog," said Heron, "you look like most other frogs to me."

"I'm called Bullfrog because I'm the mightiest frog in the swamp," Bullfrog said.

Heron only chuckled and flew down to a branch that was closer to Bullfrog's log.

What was Bullfrog going to do?

Chapter 2
Bullfrog Makes a Deal

Bullfrog decided he had to keep Heron talking. "If Heron is talking, he can't be chewing on me," he thought.

Bullfrog knew he had to think fast to outwit Heron. Suddenly, a clever idea popped into his mind.

"If you don't eat me, I will show you tomorrow night what makes me so special," he said.

"I am an expert on bullfrogs, and you look ordinary to me," laughed Heron. "You have two long legs in back and two short legs in front. You have a plump white belly and bulgy black eyes just like other bullfrogs. I can't imagine how you're any different."

Heron flew out of the tree and landed near Bullfrog. He opened and closed his long sharp bill.

CLACK! CLACK!

"Stop!" yelled Bullfrog. "Don't eat me! I promise that I am special in a way that will surprise you."

"Then why not show me right now?" asked Heron.

"I want to be sure to impress you," said Bullfrog quickly. "I want to rest up so . . . so I can show you how very special I am."

Heron began to look interested.

"I am hungry," said Heron. "But I
am also a curious bird. All right, I will
come back tomorrow. If you can show me
how special you are, I won't eat you. If not,
I'll eat you on the spot!"

Heron spread his wings. "Until tomorrow,
Bullfrog," he said. Then Heron flew away.

Chapter 3
Bullfrog Meets Butterfly

That night, Bullfrog didn't sleep a wink.

"Maybe I should leave the swamp. Maybe I should just run away," he thought. "But where would I go? I don't know anywhere else that bullfrogs can live," Bullfrog sighed.

Bullfrog thought and thought all night. Heron was sure to find him again. What could he do to prove to Heron that he was special? What new and special quality would save him?

When dawn came, a very tired Bullfrog was still sitting on his log.

The sun warmed the air.
Insects began to fly about.
Dragonflies soared through the air.
Colorful butterflies visited the flowers.
Busy bumblebees buzzed about.
Bullfrog still sat.

As Bullfrog sat on his log, he watched a brightly colored butterfly land on a flowering bush near him. The butterfly's wings fluttered gracefully as it floated from flower to flower.

"Butterfly is so pretty. If only I looked like a butterfly," Bullfrog said to himself. "Heron would be so surprised by such a gorgeous bullfrog that he would not want to eat me."

"Hello, Butterfly," said Bullfrog.

"Good morning, Bullfrog," said Butterfly from her flower. "You look very thoughtful."

"Oh, Butterfly," said Bullfrog, "my mind is working so hard this morning! I have to think of a way to make myself special for Heron. If I don't, he will eat me tonight. You look so pretty as you fly from flower to flower. Can you tell me how to make myself look as lovely as you?"

"Well," said Butterfly, "I was not always lovely. When I was a caterpillar I was fuzzy and green. I did not look very special. It wasn't until after I came out of my cocoon that I had these beautiful wings of many colors. Perhaps if you spin yourself a cocoon, you will have beautifully colored wings when you emerge."

Butterfly moved away from Bullfrog. She seemed to float around the flowers. Her beautiful, graceful wings fluttered through the air. Butterfly stopped at first one flower, then another. Her wings appeared to shimmer in the morning sun. Soon she flew away. Bullfrog was again left by himself.

Chapter 4
A Great Idea

As Bullfrog watched Butterfly fly out of sight, he thought, "Butterfly said that when she came out of her cocoon she had beautiful wings. But bullfrogs don't make cocoons. I wonder what I could do to make myself look beautiful."

Bullfrog thought and thought. Then he had an idea. He hopped off his log and down to the water's edge.

The swamp mud near the water was
yellowish in some places and reddish in
others. First, Bullfrog smeared a streak of
yellowish mud on his chest. Then, he
smeared a reddish streak of mud on his
head, under his mouth, and along each
side of his back. Finally, he made large
polka dots on his sides and back.

Bullfrog bent over to look at his reflection in the still water.

"It's not quite right," thought Bullfrog to himself. He looked around. He saw a few brightly colored feathers lying in the mud.

Bullfrog picked up a blue feather. He scooped up some reddish mud and stuck the feather onto one side of his body. Then he picked up a green feather and stuck it onto his other side with yellowish mud.

"Bullfrog," called Turtle, who had been watching, "what are you doing?"

"Oh, hello, Turtle," said Bullfrog. "I am trying to make myself look like a beautiful butterfly to impress Heron. If I can prove that I am special, Heron won't eat me."

"How do you think I look?" Bullfrog asked Turtle.

"I think you look like a bullfrog with streaks of mud, polka dots, and feathers stuck to him," replied Turtle.

Bullfrog took another look at himself in the still water.

"Oh, my, I think you're right," said Bullfrog. "I don't look beautiful at all. I look very silly. This won't work. What will I do now? Heron will surely eat me."

Bullfrog looked sadly at Turtle. Then he jumped into the water to wash off the colored mud and feathers.

Bullfrog slowly hopped back to his log.

"Turtle," asked Bullfrog, "what would you do if Heron was going to eat you?"

"Oh, herons don't eat turtles," said Turtle. "My shell is too big and hard. It is good for protection."

"What would you do if someone was *trying* to eat you?" Bullfrog asked.

"I'd pull my head and legs inside my hard shell," said Turtle slowly. "I'd keep very still. Then the someone would go away. Maybe you should grow a shell," he finished.

Turtle turned and walked slowly back to his rock.

Chapter 5
The Problem With Bullfrog's Shell

Bullfrog was left alone to think.

"I wish I had a shell like Turtle's, but how can a frog grow a shell?" thought Bullfrog to himself. Bullfrog sat on his log and thought for a long time.

"Heron would certainly not want to eat a frog with a big hard shell," he thought. "In fact, if I could pull my head and legs under the shell, Heron wouldn't even know it was me!"

Suddenly, Bullfrog had an idea. "Maybe I can make a shell. I could carry it with me all the time just like Turtle. When Heron comes, I will pull my head and legs inside my shell and be safe."

Bullfrog looked around. He saw some lily pads floating gently in the swamp. "A lily pad is the right size," thought Bullfrog, "but it is not strong enough. Heron could pull a lily pad right off with his sharp beak."

Bullfrog spotted some branches.

"Branches are strong," thought Bullfrog, "but they are not the right shape. The branches are long and thin. I am short and wide. Heron would see me right through the branches, and I would be his dinner!"

Bullfrog looked on the ground for
something else to use to make a shell.
Everything near the swamp was wet and
soggy. Then Bullfrog looked in the woods
away from the water. Everything there was
soft and green. He looked up into the
treetops. Everything was so far away. Then
Bullfrog spotted something that might work.

"If I could get that nest, I could make myself a shell," said Bullfrog. "If only I could reach it."

Just then, Squirrel hopped onto the branch.

"Squirrel," called Bullfrog, "could you knock that old nest out of the tree for me?"

"Why do you want this old nest?" asked Squirrel.

"I want to use it to make myself a shell like Turtle's. Then Heron will think I am special, and he won't eat me for dinner," answered Bullfrog.

"If you really want this old nest, stand under the tree," said Squirrel. "I will try to make the nest land on your back."

Bullfrog hopped over to the trunk of the tree. He sat right below the nest.

"Squirrel," called Bullfrog, "I'm all ready. But maybe you should practice first. You might miss."

Squirrel looked around for something to use as a test. Then she spotted an acorn.

"I'll use this acorn," she said. "Here it comes."

Squirrel aimed for the middle of Bullfrog's back. The acorn landed on Bullfrog's head with a sharp KERPLUNK!

Squirrel picked another acorn. She
aimed again for the middle of Bullfrog's
back. This time the acorn landed in the
right place and rolled right off.

"Good," said Bullfrog. "Try the nest."

Squirrel gave a mighty shove. The nest
sailed through the air and landed upside
down, right on Bullfrog's back.

Bullfrog's head and neck stuck out from under the nest, just like Turtle's did from his shell. The nest seemed hard and strong, and it fit perfectly on Bullfrog's back.

Bullfrog spent several hours walking around with his shell on his back. He practiced pulling his head and legs under the nest for protection. For a while, Bullfrog thought he had finally found a way to outwit Heron.

Bullfrog climbed back onto his log wearing his new shell and a big smile. The sun beat down on Bullfrog's head. It beat down on the nest on his back.

Bullfrog began to feel very warm. The nest was heavy and hot. The scratchy twigs next to Bullfrog's dry skin were beginning to make him feel very itchy.

"Maybe I will take a quick dip in the water," said Bullfrog. "Turtle goes in the water all the time."

Bullfrog leaped into the water. It felt so good to be wet again!

Suddenly, he felt pieces of the nest getting soft and mushy. He saw chunks of mud and many twigs floating around him.

"Oh, no!" cried Bullfrog. "My shell is floating away!"

When the nest had touched the water, the hard, dry mud had turned into soft, mushy mud. The twigs and leaves had loosened and floated away. Bullfrog's skin was no longer itchy, but his shell was gone!

Chapter 6
Dragonfly's Big Idea

Bullfrog sat on his log. The sun moved across the sky. The air became still in the hazy afternoon. Thirsty animals came to the swamp to drink. He was still deep in thought on his log.

"Butterfly is special because she has such beautiful colors," he thought. "Turtle has a shell that is special. But I still can't think of anything that is special about me. Heron's belly will be full tonight unless I do something that shows how special I am!"

Bullfrog slowly became aware of a soft whirring sound. Out of the corner of his eye, he saw a glint that appeared to hang in the air overhead. It was Dragonfly. The late afternoon sun was making his pale wings sparkle and shine.

"Dragonfly, I need your help," called out Bullfrog. "Will you please come talk to me?"

"Good afternoon, Bullfrog," said Dragonfly. "If I come closer you might eat me. So I think I'll stay just where I am." He started to fly away.

"Oh, no, Dragonfly. I am much too concerned about being Heron's dinner to be hungry," Bullfrog sighed.

"Bullfrog," said Dragonfly, still flying a safe distance away. "What's wrong?"

Bullfrog told Dragonfly the whole story of how Heron would come to eat him.

"I understand your problem," said Dragonfly. "But I don't know how I can help."

Bullfrog looked at Dragonfly, admiring his pale wings.

"Dragonfly," said Bullfrog, "how did you get your wings?"

"I've had wings for as long as I can remember," Dragonfly replied.

"If I had silky wings, I could fly away from Heron," said Bullfrog. "But bullfrogs are not born with wings."

"You could make wings," said Dragonfly.

"Where in the swamp will I find what I need to make wings?" asked Bullfrog doubtfully.

"Why don't you ask some of the birds?" suggested Dragonfly. "Maybe Hummingbird or Chickadee could help you."

"Hummingbird and Chickadee are busy using their wings to fly around all over the swamp," said Bullfrog. "I doubt they would ever stop long enough to tell me how I could make wings."

"Well, I'm sorry, Bullfrog, but I don't have any better idea. Goodbye," Dragonfly called as he flew off into the early evening sky.

"Goodbye," called Bullfrog.

Again, Bullfrog was left alone on his log to think about how to solve his problem.

Chapter 7
If Bullfrogs Had Wings

"Where could I get what I need to make wings?" thought Bullfrog.

As tired as he was, Bullfrog would not give up. He decided to take a hop to clear his mind and to think.

Bullfrog started to hop down.

"Don't step on me!" squeaked a voice from below.

Bullfrog peered over the end of his log.

There was Spider sitting in the middle of
a large web that was attached to one end
of Bullfrog's log. Spider's web was shiny
and silky. It reminded Bullfrog of
something. But what?

"Of course!" Bullfrog thought. "Spider's
web looks a lot like Dragonfly's wings."

47

"Spider," said Bullfrog excitedly, "Heron plans on having me for dinner tonight unless I can prove to him that I am special."

"I heard you talking to Dragonfly just now," said Spider. "How can I help you?"

"The silk in your web reminds me of Dragonfly's wings. If I had wings, I would be special. Do you think you could help me make wings?" Bullfrog asked.

"I'd like to help you make wings," said Spider, "but when I spin my webs, I need something to attach them to. That is why I'm using the end of your log," said Spider.

"So I need something that is shaped like the edge of a wing. Then you can attach the thread to the edge and spin your thread inside it," said Bullfrog.

"Where are you going to find something that is wing-shaped?" wondered Spider.

Bullfrog looked around him. He saw marsh grass growing, but marsh grass was tall and skinny. He saw a cattail, but cattails were round and puffy.

Then Bullfrog saw a leaf that had fallen off an elm tree that was growing close by. The leaf was fat in the middle and pointy on one end. On the other end a long strong stem was sticking out.

Bullfrog took a closer look. The stem of the elm leaf was strong.

"Maybe I can tear away the inside of each leaf and leave the stem. I bet Spider can attach her thread to the stem," thought Bullfrog.

Bullfrog looked at the setting sun.

"It's getting late. I've got to work fast," he thought. "Heron will be back soon."

Bullfrog carefully tore away the soft green part of two leaves. He brought what was left of the leaves back to Spider.

"Spider, start spinning," said Bullfrog, "and please hurry!"

Soon Spider had filled in the leaves with her silky web. Then she used a strand of silk to hop onto Bullfrog's back. In a moment, she had the wings firmly attached.

"Oh, thank you, Spider," said Bullfrog. "You can always use my log for your web."

Bullfrog hopped away, looking for a place to test his wings. As he hopped, his wings bounced up and down on his back. He was looking for something that was tall enough so that when he hopped off, he would be able to flap his wings and fly.

"Heron will be amazed to see me flying away," thought Bullfrog.

Bullfrog hopped onto a tall rock near the water. His wings felt light and strong on his back. He moved to the edge of the rock and looked down.

"Here I go!" shouted Bullfrog as he leaped off the rock.

For a moment the wings held Bullfrog up. But Bullfrog was too big and heavy. The wings were too light and airy.

With a plop and a thud, Bullfrog fell headfirst into the mud. The wings broke away from his body and floated, light as a feather, to the ground beside him.

As the sun slowly set, Bullfrog knew that he was running out of time.

Chapter 8
The End of Bullfrog?

Bullfrog knew that the end was near. He had tried as hard as he could to make himself special. He could not make himself look as beautiful as Butterfly. He could not make himself a strong shell for protection like Turtle's. His dragonfly wings were a failure.

As Bullfrog crawled back onto his log, he could see a bird flying toward him.

"I tried all day to make myself special," said Bullfrog, "but nothing worked. Why am I the only one who isn't special?"

Bullfrog thought to himself, "I guess I'll never find out. Heron is on his way."

As Bullfrog watched Heron getting closer and closer, he realized that he wasn't just scared. He was getting angry! He wasn't going to be any bird's dinner!

Bullfrog sat up straight and tall on his log, waiting for Heron. As Heron flew closer and closer, Bullfrog took a deep breath. He reached way down deep inside himself, right down to his toes. He took a long breath and held it for a moment.

Then he pulled out a sound that he had never made before. The sound vibrated through the swamp. It sounded like music from a bass fiddle. It was long and low, and it was VERY loud, like thunder rolling across the swamp.

"JUG-O-ROOM!" Bullfrog bellowed. The sound echoed through the swamp.

"JUG-O-ROOM!" he bellowed again.

The sound surprised Bullfrog. The sound also surprised many other animals.

The one who was most surprised was Heron, who was just about to land on Bullfrog's log. In fact, Heron was so surprised that he almost fell out of the air.

"Bullfrog!" Heron began in a voice that was a bit shaky. "I see what you mean about being a special frog."

Bullfrog took another deep breath. He was just about to bellow again when Heron quickly interrupted.

"Bullfrog, I beg you. Please stop!" cried Heron. "I can see that you truly are a VERY special bullfrog," said Heron nervously. "Maybe I will look for a smaller bullfrog to eat for dinner. I'll find one that has a smaller sound, too!"

With those words, Heron flew away.

"Wow!" thought Bullfrog. "I never knew I could make a sound like that. I was special all along and didn't know it."

With Heron gone, Bullfrog became quiet.
Peace returned to the swamp at last.
All the animals went back to doing what
they usually do at night in the swamp.

A very tired Bullfrog settled himself on
his log. Above him the moon was full and
bright. All around him he heard the familiar
sounds of animals getting ready for
the night.

All of the pleasant swamp sounds made
Bullfrog feel calm and happy. With a smile
on his face, Bullfrog closed his eyes. Then
he peacefully drifted off to sleep.

GLOSSARY

cocoon (kuh KOON) a case made of a silky thread that caterpillars spin around themselves to protect them while they change into butterflies or moths

concerned (kun SURND) worried, uneasy

echo (EK oh) sound heard again when sound waves bounce off of a surface

emerge (ee MURJ) to come out of

failure (FAYL yur) the act of not succeeding or not doing

impress (ihm PRES) to have an effect on someone's thinking or feelings

ordinary (ORD ihn er ee) normal; not special in any way

outwit (owt WIHT) to win by being smarter or more clever

reflection (rih FLEK shun) an image thrown back by a surface such as a mirror or still water

vibrated (VYE brayt ihd) moved quickly back and forth; echoed